There's an "A" in Every mAn

Dr. Larry D. Johnson

J. Kenkade
PUBLISHING®
LITTLE ROCK, ARKANSAS

J. Kenkade Publishing
6104 Forbing Rd
Little Rock, AR 72209
www.jkenkadepublishing.com
Facebook.com/jkenkadepublishing

J. Kenkade Publishing is a registered trademark.

Printed in the United States of America
ISBN 978-1-944486-97-6

The views expressed in this book are those of the author and do not necessarily reflect the views of Publisher.

There's an "A" in Every mAn

Dedication

I would like to thank my loving wife Attorney Holly Johnson and my precious daughter Karrington NiKole Johnson for supporting me continuously the past couple of years while I was writing my book. I also want to give thanks to my sister Dr. Fannie Johnson Albert for her unselfish support. Thanks to all of my friends and family for their support. Thanks to my good friend Ricky "Elder" Jackson for listening to my many ideas every week about my book. Thanks to my Fellowship Missionary Baptist Church Family.

I would like to dedicate this book to my sons Raco and DeLerick, as well as all men. May God bless all that read this book.

Table of Contents

PREFACE

In writing this book, it is my desire to serve as a beacon of light to anyone who finds themselves in a dark place in life, especially men who find it challenging to just be themselves. I was motivated to write this book after volunteering as a teacher in a local prison for an entire year. I was privileged to teach a lesson entitled "Iron Sharpens Iron". This was a class where men were taught how to build each other up and understand it's okay to support each other. There were times I was in the presence of two hundred men in one setting. That's when it dawned on me that no matter our respective physical sizes, all of our hearts are nearly the same. The average size of a heart is about the size of a fist, weighing around ten pounds. My point is that all men have a soft spot in their hearts somewhere. It just takes the right person to find it.

Hopefully, this book will ignite a thirst that can only be quenched by studying and reading more. My heart yearns daily for men to see themselves the way that God sees them. I am sure that so many grew up in unbalanced homes, which led to unbalanced behaviors. Yes, I get it, if you were raised in a home where you either saw violence or experienced it on a daily basis, your response to life's evolving changes, situations, and circumstances will more than likely be different than the response of someone who did not. If you grew up in a home where yelling, cursing, and screaming were the norm, then your response to authoritative figures will definitely be different.

No matter what hand life has dealt, I want men to understand that their environments and backgrounds do not have to negatively impact their futures or define their successes in life. We have choices. So, it's up to us to choose the road we travel, considering that all roads lead somewhere. Trust me, if you didn't have anything to offer, Satan would not be after you. He is actually after what's on the inside of you–your greatness. I have come to the realization that there is an "A" inside of every man. No man is perfect, but with the right motivation and courage, he can definitely strive for perfection.

If you were raised in a home where you either saw violence day in and day out or perhaps you grew up in a home where destructive words were an everyday meal or perhaps yelling, cussing and screaming were the norm, I get it. Regardless of the situation, we must now be accountable for our actions.

In my book, I used the letter "A" that's found in the center of "man" to remind you that every man has an "A" in him. Secondly, I used the letter "A" because that's how we express the best of the best in the USA. Our school system uses the letter "A" to signify excellence. Just like our grades in the school system, so is it in real life. Even if you make a D or an F, it's not the end of life. It's the beginning of working your butt off to do better next time.

Sometimes we fail in life; we make an F. We give thanks to God that an F doesn't stand for "final" or "finished". Just as it is in school, when you receive an F, you have to work extremely hard to get it removed. Likewise, in life, whenever (notice I said when and not if) you make an F on this journey, you must work just as hard to get back in the game.

Now that we know what all the hype is about with the "A", we can focus on becoming everything God has designed us to become. Don't let the enemy push you to the edge.

Take a time-out. Learn to walk away. Don't try to get the last word in. Go for a walk.

Go for a jog. Go to the park. Take a ride around the block. Go see a movie. Here's my favorite response: "Okay!"

This is not a "black or white" book. It's a book for whoever can benefit from reading it. It is my prayer that men and women will read and share this book with their family members, especially those who can't seem to shake off past pain and problems that keep hunting them day in and day out.

Chapter 1:

NO MORE EXCUSES

"And Moses said unto the Lord, O my Lord, I am not eloquent, neither heretofore, nor since thou hast spoken unto thy servant: but I am slow of speech, and of a slow tongue."
Exodus 4:10

So many of us are like Moses, who had an excuse for why he didn't want to do what the Lord had called him to do. It is the common denominator that we all share: excuses, excuses, excuses. We could all make excuses as to why things are the way they are in our lives. We could make excuses for every failure or setback in our lives. Yes, some of the things that happen in our lives are just mishaps and often land us in compromising positions. However, most of the unsuccessful roads that we travel are roads we chose in spite of all the warning signs.

We could all make excuses for why we are not successful. Many of us will blame others for the outcomes of our lives. While there might be a degree of validity to that, at the end of the day, the fact remains that we are where we are regardless of who is at fault. All of us must come to the place of accountability. Once you and I take responsibility for our own lives, we can strategically start making plans to move forward.

In the verse above, Moses begins to give God excuses for why he can't do what God asked him to do. Like Moses, at one point or another, all of us have been guilty of making excuses for something we didn't want to do. Making excuses is the typical behavior displayed when we are not ready to step up and take responsibility for our actions. Regardless of whether we are at fault or if we've been falsely accused, either way, life must go on. We must continue moving forward. I tell my congregation often that if a man falls forward, he has gained something, and a man that is always sitting down never has to worry about falling down. No one is ever proud of their mistakes, but we can't afford to spend days feeling sorry for ourselves. Yes, repent, be remorseful, and get back up. But, by all means, you can't quit.

Notice what happens here in Genesis 3:1-17:

"Now the serpent was more subtil than any beast of the field which the Lord God had made. And he said unto the woman, Yea, hath God said, Ye shall not eat of every tree of the garden? And the woman said unto the serpent, we may eat of the fruit of the trees of the garden: But of the fruit of the tree which is in the midst of the garden, God hath said, Ye shall not eat of it, neither shall ye touch it, lest ye die. And the serpent said unto the woman, Ye shall not surely die: For God doth know that in the day ye eat thereof, then your eyes shall be opened, and ye shall be as gods, knowing good and evil. And when the woman saw that the tree was good for food, and that it was pleasant to the eyes, and a tree to be desired to make one wise, she took of the fruit thereof, and did eat, and gave also unto her husband with her; and he did eat. And the eyes of them both were opened, and they knew that they were naked; and they sewed fig leaves together, and made themselves aprons. And they heard the voice of the Lord God walking in the garden in the cool of the day: and Adam and his wife hid themselves from the presence of the Lord God amongst the trees of the garden. And the Lord God called unto Adam, and said unto him, Where art thou? And he said, I heard thy voice in the garden, and I was afraid, because I was naked; and I hid myself. And he said, who told thee

that thou wast naked? Hast thou eaten of the tree, whereof I commanded thee that thou shouldest not eat? And the man said, The woman whom thou gavest to be with me, she gave me of the tree, and I did eat. And the Lord God said unto the woman, What is this that thou hast done? And the woman said, The serpent beguiled me, and I did eat. And the Lord God said unto the serpent, Because thou hast done this, thou art cursed above all cattle, and above every beast of the field; upon thy belly shalt thou go, and dust shalt thou eat all the days of thy life: And I will put enmity between thee and the woman, and between thy seed and her seed; it shall bruise thy head, and thou shalt bruise his heel. Unto the woman he said, I will greatly multiply thy sorrow and thy conception; in sorrow thou shalt bring forth children; and thy desire shall be to thy husband, and he shall rule over thee. And unto Adam he said, Because thou hast hearkened unto the voice of thy wife, and hast eaten of the tree, of which I commanded thee, saying, Thou shalt not eat of it: cursed is the ground for thy sake; in sorrow shalt thou eat of it all the days of thy life..."

Notice in these verses above that no one takes the blame. It becomes a "she said, he said" battle. The man (Adam) says the woman God gave to be with him gave him of the tree. The man blames God for giving him the woman to deceive him. He blames God and the woman for his disobedience. The woman says the serpent beguiled ("charmed" or "tricked") her to eat the fruit. They both admit they did eat the fruit, but neither takes the blame. Isn't this just like us, always wanting to blame others for our failures and mishaps in life? If you continue reading the remainder of the chapter, you will notice that God addresses each one of them for their disobedient acts. My point is: yes, God is loving, kind, gracious and faithful, but He does not blink at sin; neither will sin go unpunished. God dealt with each of them for their sin.

The point I want to make is whenever we sin against the Almighty God, there will always be repercussions. The Word of God makes it clear that "the wages of sin is death" (Romans 6:23). There is always a high price for sin. Again, we must acknowledge our sin, confess our sin, and repent of our sins. Then, our God will forgive us of our sins. As long as we hide our sin, we can never be healed of our sin. Lying and covering up are the same as hiding our sin. The sooner we come clean with God, the better off we'll be, meaning we can begin the healing process.

I am reminded of another God-fearing man in the Bible who came up with an excuse as to why he couldn't do what God had called him to do.

Exodus 4:10-16 reveals to us the excuse Moses gives:

"And Moses said unto the Lord, O my Lord, I am not eloquent, neither heretofore, nor since thou hast spoken unto thy servant: but I am slow of speech, and of a slow tongue. And the Lord said unto him, Who hath made man's mouth? or who maketh the dumb, or deaf, or the seeing, or the blind? have not I the Lord? Now therefore go, and I will be with thy mouth, and teach thee what thou shalt say. And he said, O my Lord, send, I pray thee, by the hand of him whom thou wilt send. And the anger of the Lord was kindled against Moses, and he said, Is not Aaron the Levite thy brother? I know that he can speak well. And also, behold, he cometh forth to meet thee: and when he seeth thee, he will be glad in his heart. And thou shalt speak unto him, and put words in his mouth: and I will be with thy mouth, and with his mouth, and will teach you what ye shall do. And he shall be thy spokesman unto the people: and he shall be to thee instead of a mouth, and thou shalt be to him instead of God."

Again, another man who God chose to use made an excuse for why he wasn't the right man for the job. What he didn't realize was that God already knew how he would sound before Moses knew himself. My reason for using Adam and Moses is not to try to show them up, but instead to show them off. God doesn't necessarily call who is qualified. He qualifies who He calls. These are men God used at the beginning of time to do some awesome work. I am totally convinced that God can use whomever He chooses. There was only one perfect person who ever lived, and that was God's Son, Jesus. Everyone else just thinks they are. That's why they are always judging others.

What we are to learn from this lesson is when we obey God, He can use us to accomplish great things. However, when we try to do it without him, we are going to fail every time. Yes, scripture tells us that we can do all things through Him that gives us strength. Likewise, in the verses you just finished reading, God never asked Moses how well he could speak. He wasn't looking to see how well he could speak. He was looking to see how well he could obey. You see, we are always doing things backwards. We are always trying to tell God what we can't do and why we're not able to do it instead of saying, "Yes, Lord, I will obey." God showed me years ago that any time a person does not follow instructions, there will always be destruction.

So many of us are where we are simply because we didn't follow God's instructions. It can be devastating when we don't follow His instructions, but as soon as destruction arises, we want Him to follow our instruction to deliver us immediately. Well, it doesn't exactly work that way, but thank God for His amazing grace and everlasting mercies that are renewed every morning. Even when we make mistakes, God can take them and turn them around and let them work for good. He's just that kind of God. He can take a mess and turn it into an awesome message. However, scripture teaches us not to tempt the Lord.

Instead of making excuses, I think it would be a good idea if we would simply excuse ourselves. In other words, get out of God's way and learn how to follow where He leads us. For so many, it is much easier to come up with an excuse instead of executing. I learned from first-hand experience that it's a lot easier in the long run to just do it and do it right the first time.

Instead of worrying about messing up, we need to trust that God is actually setting us up–yes, setting us up to be blessed. There is always a blessing in obedience. We must realize that, ultimately, all that we do should be focused on bringing God glory. That means sometimes we might be laughed at and other times we might be looked at. It really doesn't matter how we sound. I'd much rather be doing right than sounding right any day. God is always looking for someone who will obey. We should never seek to please people at the expense of displeasing our Maker and Creator. After all, scripture teaches us that only what we do for Christ will last.

God isn't necessarily looking for the best; He's looking for someone who's willing to give their best. You might not look like anything or sound like anything to the world. But I can promise you God accepts obedience over sound and looks any day of the week. We have to do like the prodigal son; scriptures teach us that he came to himself. In other words, he realized he was nothing without God but everything with God. I challenge you as you read this book to make up your mind and surrender to the will of God, and He will give you a life that you could have never dreamed of. Think about it: what do you have to lose trusting God? You've tried everything under the sun, and nothing has afforded you the results you were hoping for.

I am a living witness that if you surrender to the will of God, He will literally take you places and give you things you couldn't have ever imagined. Who else do you know who rewards you for doing what you should be doing anyway?

Chapter 2:

SHAKE IT OFF

"And he shook off the beast into
the fire, and felt no harm."
Acts 28:5

In the above chapter of Acts, Paul (along with 275 other prisoners) is being carried to Rome to stand trial before Caesar. Paul is basically going to stand trial for preaching the gospel. At the beginning of this particular story, back in chapter 27, Paul warns Julius, the centurion of Augustus' band, that it is a bad time to sail. Julius is eager to present Paul before Caesar until he realizes Caesar isn't willing to listen to anything Paul or anyone else has to say. Thus, they begin to sail, despite it not being a good time of year, and a tempestuous wind called Euroclydon arises against the ship. Euroclydon is a strong windstorm, somewhat like a typhoon, that can toss ships around as if no one is on them.

The storm is so bad that the ship eventually crashes and lands on an island called Melita. When the barbarous people saw Paul and the others, they were very kind, so they were willing to make them a fire to get warm. Paul, being a doer, was helping put wood on the fire when he reached to get a bundle of wood, and a viper (a venomous snake) fastened to his hand. The Bible says in Acts 28:5 that Paul shook the beast off into the fire and felt no harm. This is letting you know that whatever has bitten you in life doesn't have to kill you if you learn how to shake it off and move forward with your life.

It is very important to learn how to shake stuff off wherever it happened and not carry it through life. You'll be able to better understand this contextually as you continue to read.

I've come to realize as we traverse through this world that there are countless things in life that we'll have to shake off. I preached a sermon at my church one Sunday morning and used this verse as one of my key verses. I titled the sermon "How to Win with a Bad Hand", referring to the "bad hand" you might play during a card game like Spades. Spades is a game where you literally have to play with the hand you're dealt. Of course, in this game, the more spades you have in most cases, the better off you are. However, there are cases where you can play an excellent game with only a couple of spades, providing your partner has a few spades to back you up. In each suit of cards, there's an Ace, King, Queen and Jack of Spades, clubs, diamonds and hearts. You can still do well if you are dealt the Ace and King of each suit, providing other players have a couple of each. The point is, although the name of the game is Spades, it's possible to survive without many and sometimes any.

At the end of the day, you must play the hand you're dealt.

This is also true for your life, regardless of your parents, where they were born, where you were born, your educational background, your job status, and so on. I like to put it this way: we're here now. Big deal, your father wasn't around; you're here now. Big deal, your mom wasn't around; you're here now. Big deal, you were adopted, raised in the projects, raised on welfare, raised by a single parent, or raised in the country (so was I).

As a matter of fact, not only was I raised in the country, but I also lived as deep in the country as anyone I was raised around. We lived so far off the main roads that there wasn't another house on the other side of ours. When you passed our home, there was nothing but woods and wildlife. At any given time at night, you could hear a panther, or you may see a fox or coyote. Even a bear or two could be spotted.

If you were to go to where I was raised today, you would see there are only two houses still standing in the entire community called Jones Ridge. Allow me to inform you that when I grew up there, there were at least five or six small grocery stores, two churches, one store in the daytime, and a juke joint (small night club) at night. It took two buses to pick up all the school kids. There were at least 45 to 50 homes in our community throughout.

I grew up off what was called the "Big Road" (simply put: a long, graveled road). I had to walk nearly half a mile from down in the field to catch the bus each morning. On days when it was raining, it was the worst. Not only did I have to run to the bus in the rain, but when I finally got to the bus, no one wanted me to sit with them because I was wet. It was horrible to be laughed at and talked about, but I survived (by the grace of God and my mother's prayers). I am the ninth child, the youngest since my baby sister passed last year. So, it was all Mother could do just to provide for us to go to school.

It was a very difficult and challenging time for me. You have no idea how many paddlings I receive for not having my homework, and most of the time, it was because I didn't have anything to write with and nothing to write on. Many times,

I had to erase something off my paper to reuse it or try to borrow from my classmate. There were four or five of my classmates who knew of my situation and were always willing to help me.

I'll never forget all the days I was laughed at and made fun of because of what I had on or how nappy my hair was or how much grease I had on my face. There was just always something for the "well-to-do" kids to laugh at. I remember this one classmate – I won't use his name, although he got killed in a car accident several years ago. His parents had good jobs and kept him well-dressed. Alternatively, I had a shoestring around my waist to use as a belt. I had on mismatched socks. I remember on one occasion I had a pair of shoes so worn and ragged that I tore a piece of our ragged linoleum off the floor and put it in the bottom of my shoe to keep my foot from being on the floor.

So, yes, this boy was able to wear whatever he wanted. He had on something new nearly every week and didn't mind letting you know. He would get a laugh at my expense almost every other day until I changed buses.

We had chickens and hogs that I had to feed (we called it "slopping the hogs") every evening after school, I had to chop wood and put wood on the porch every evening after school (yes, that means we had a wood heater to keep warm by). I had to pump water every evening for the night (yes, that means we had a well pump). Mother woke up me, my sisters who are a couple years older than me, and my baby sister (Gloria, who recently passed on April 13, 2019) on Saturday mornings so we could pump (hand pump) wash water. "Hand pump" means we had to pump water in a bucket and poor it in the washing machine until it was full in order to wash colored clothes. We had to pump more water to put in a black iron kettle, which was heated by a wood fire and poured in the washing machine for white clothes. It was so hard getting up early on Saturday mornings after staying up late Friday nights.

I had to get what was called the "night pan" each night and empty it each morning. We didn't have indoor plumbing. More specifically, we didn't have an inside toilet. Therefore, we used a night pan with a top on it. I had to walk two to three miles one way to the local grocery store, often times in the rain, to get what Mother needed. My mom and dad did not ever own a vehicle. By this time, my older brother and sister had moved away.

As I was old enough, I had to go to the cotton field to chop cotton. Can you believe I chopped cotton (the grass not the actual cotton) for only $5.00 per day? Let's do the math. I was in the field at 7:00am (with a one-hour lunch break) until 6:00pm, and my mother received $5.00 for me chopping cotton for that day. Yep. You guessed right. I received $25.00 for a week's work. Well, actually, for 50 hours. That comes to around 50 cents an hour (and you're complaining about your salary?)

I also had to pick cotton on weekends with my mother when the cotton was ready for picking. The farmer would let Mother have what was called "scrap cotton" to use to make quilts. Yep, you guessed right again; my mother sewed quilts to keep us warm during the winter months. I also chopped beans (the grass, not the actual beans). When you chop beans, unlike cotton, you walk down the center of the row and chop the inside of the row on your left and the row on your right. With cotton, the entire row is your responsibility.

I worked in the rice field putting in levy gates, and I worked at the cotton gin. I did what was called "spot chopping". This is where you walk across the field to chop a particular weed. In most cases, it was Johnson Grass, a weed with leaves nearly as sharp as a razor.

I'll make this my last one, although there's more. When I was around 12 or 13, I would mow my neighbor's yard for 50 cents. She was an elderly lady. In addition to her yard, she wanted me to mow a path to the outdoor toilet, which was away from the house. She wanted a path so she could get to her garden, as well as around the shed out back. When I turned 15 years old,

I asked her for a raise. I asked her if she could pay me one dollar. She promptly fired me and hired another young boy in the neighborhood.

Now, this is what it's like to play with the hand you're dealt. Oh, I forgot to mention that my mom and dad separated when I was two (according to my older siblings). Just in case you're grown and still whining about who wasn't there, now it's your responsibility. It's called accountability. Thank God they were around long enough to get you here.

You and I can't spend our entire lives blaming everybody else for where we are at this point. I always wondered why people always blame their failures on other people but then also claim their own success? For example, if we don't know how to do something or don't achieve something, we blame our parent or say that no one ever showed us the way to do a certain thing. But check this out – our parents didn't teach us how to lie, steal, have sex, rob, break in, sell drugs, rap, shack up, use cell phones, wear our pants down, cuss, fuss, fight, and so on. I think you get my point. We learn what we want to learn, and for what we don't want to learn, we find someone to blame.

My encouragement to all of you is to let the past go (shake it off), accept full responsibility for your own life, and be willing to be accountable for your own actions. Pray and ask God for guidance. I promise you that He will direct your path whenever you're ready to stop doing things your way and acknowledge that you're ready to follow Him.

Unfortunately, you'll have to shake off countless things in this life. The Bible teaches us that many are the afflictions of the righteous, but God delivers us from them all. There you have it. Although you and I are made righteous by the blood of Jesus, we also will have many unpleasant circumstances in this life.

Remember: because of the sin-cursed world we now live in, every person is born in sin and shaped in iniquity.

Thank God for the good news, though. Jesus paid a hefty price for our sins. Therefore, you and I don't have to walk around with a heavy burden. We can repent of our sins, shake it off, and live a glorious and victorious life.

This is the very reason I wanted to get this book in your hand. I know the trick of the enemy; it is to kill a brother's dream, steal a brother's joy, and destroy every good thought. Satan wants you to stay in your defeated place. He does this by reminding you daily of the things you did in life to get you in an unpleasant position. Thank God you don't have to stay in the shape you're in. Furthermore, your failure does not have to be final.

Sin or bad decisions are never to be taken lightly. When we recognize we have sinned, we must move to repentance with haste. It is not my intention to minimize sin, but rather to let you know you don't have to stay in the shape you're in. If you don't know where to start in order to move forward, start by asking the Lord Jesus to show you the way. It's okay to be open, honest, and vulnerable before God. He welcomes you to bring all of your problems, cares, and concerns to Him. Fathers want to help their children enjoy their best lives. The same is true for our Heavenly Father. He wants you to have victory in every area of your life.

Listen, I've come up short so many times, but my God has always made up the difference. Not only did God make up the difference, but the truth is that He is the difference. I'm not sure how much you know about the Word of God. Don't let the interchanging uses of "God", "Jesus", "Father", "Lord", "Savior" and "the Holy Ghost" confuse you. They are all one. The Word of God lets us know that the Father, Son, and Holy Ghost are one. I know there are several different names and titles. Actually, there are so many more, and that can be a bit confusing if you're trying to figure out who these different people are and what their assignments are. So, to keep it simple, you can call Him Jesus or God. As you continue to grow in the Word, the Holy Ghost will reveal to you the meaning of the different names and their responsibilities.

The main thing I want to convey is that we serve a forgiving God. I want to let you know that God sent His Son to this sin-sick world to die for all of our sins. Not forgiving yourself can have you just as weighed down as the sin itself can. Sin will destroy you, and unforgiveness will cause you to destroy yourself.

Satan wants us to kill each other out of anger, pursuit of self-gain, and foolishness. The destruction and self-destruction I see on television, internet, newspaper, and so on every day are what started the fire in me to write this particular book. I noticed how police officers were shooting and killing black brothers as if they were out in the woods hunting wildlife, and that was disturbing to me. I also noticed how we were shooting and killing each other, clearly not taking into account or considering that each person killed is someone's son, brother, father, uncle, nephew, grandfather, great grandfather, cousin, stepdad, or husband. The list goes on and on.

I knew I had to write this book. It is my hope and prayer that every male, especially every black male, would take the time to read it. I have a heart for all men and women. It's just that I noticed how senseless black-on-black crime is and wanted to address my concern.

Each time a brother is killed, I feel like a part of me is being murdered. So many men and women have died and sacrificed so we could have various rights and freedom. It saddens my heart to see us self-destruct. I understand that people sometimes push us to the edge, but there has to be another way to resolve the issue without killing somebody's son. We must realize that a woman carried this child for nine (give or take) long months and that if no one else loves or wants this person, their mother and father do.

Every life is important to God. God has a plan for all of our lives. His plan for us is peace and not evil. He plans to navigate us to our expected end. My way of saying, "There's an A in every man!" is that there is greatness in every man. It is crystal clear to me that if every man understood his worth, he wouldn't devalue another man. Every man wants to be successful and respected. However, every man must also understand that both success and respect are earned.

I have watched too many brothers travel down the same road and end up in the same place. I am in no way saying that I haven't made mistakes or have made all the right decisions because I have not. What I am saying is that God had mercy and delivered me, and He'll do the same for you. God has a plan for each of us if we are willing to throw our hands up and surrender to Him.

I must admit, His plan usually isn't an overnight success. Just for the record, He can make you successful overnight if He chooses to. Most of the time, God grants us things according to our spiritual maturity. God's success is different from man's success. Man thinks success is having a lot of money and a lot of stuff. In God's eyes, we are successful when we surrender our lives to Him and follow where He leads us.

Chapter 3:

You Don't Have to Look Like What You've Been through

"And the princes, governors, and captains, and the king's counsellors, being gathered together, saw these men, upon whose bodies the fire had no power, nor was a hair of their head singed, neither were their coats changed, nor the smell of fire had passed on them."
Daniel 3:27

There's a great lesson to be learned from these three faithful men of God. I trust that after reading about these men, you are able to walk with confidence like never before. These four young men are referred to as Daniel, Shadrach, Meshach, and Abednego. These young men were captured by the Babylonian invaders along with other Hebrews and taken back to Babylon to serve King Nebuchadnezzar. When these young men arrived in Babylon, their names were changed from Daniel, Hananiah, Mishael, and Azariah to Belteshazzar, Shadrach, Meshach, and Abednego. They were given these names because Hebrew names had religious significance, as each name spoke about the God of Israel.

This chapter highlights that someone might put numbers on your back and change your name, but that doesn't mean you have to change your game. Let's take a look at what their names were changed to but didn't change them.

Daniel's name means: "God is my judge". His name was changed to "Belteshazzar", which means: "Bel is my judge". Bel is the name of one of the Babylonians gods. Hananiah's name means: "God is gracious". His name was changed to "Shadrach", which means: "illuminated by the sun god". Mishael's name means: "who is like God?" His name was changed to "Meshach", which means: "who is like Venus?" Azariah's name means: "the Lord is my helper". His name was changed to "Abednego", which means: "the worshipper of Nego". Nego was the Babylonian god of wisdom.

I wanted to point this out because someone reading this might be in a place of confinement, perhaps a jail or prison or some other institution where they address you by number (and, in some cases, might even give you a new name). I want it to resonate in your spirit that there's an "A" inside of you. The letter "A" in my book represents excellence. In America, an "A" is the highest grade you can achieve.

My spiritual assignment is to remind every man, as well as every woman, of the greatness God has placed inside of them. It amazes me that God created all of us differently. Even though identical twins look alike, they have different fingerprints and a number of other differences.

So many people fall into the trap of identifying with the names they are called. Just because someone calls you a punk, you don't have to become one. Just because someone calls you sorry, you don't have to receive that. Just because someone calls you no good, low down, good for nothing, lazy, the b-word, or any of the other names I didn't list, you don't have to succumb to any of them. As a matter of fact, learn to use the negative things people say to bring out the best in you. We were always taught that it's not what you're called– it's what you answer to.

When I was in high school, we had an annual yearbook. In that yearbook were a number of titles, such as "best dressed", "most likely to succeed", "biggest flirt", "most athletic", and many others I can't remember. The point I'm making is that many, if not most, did not live up to the titles that that were chosen by others. On the other hand, many of us surpassed what others thought we were. God showed me a long time ago that if I never got my name recorded in any yearbook or any other book, it didn't matter as long as my name was recorded in His book of life. Being an old country boy wearing "hand-me-down" clothes, I was like many others. I didn't see myself living the life I now live. It doesn't matter what others call you. Like I said, I've always been told, "It isn't what they call you – it's what you answer to."

This is kind of like the young men in the book of Daniel. It's in chapter three that we gain divine insight on how not to look like we've been through what we've been through. Believe it or not, these four young men were at one time elevated to places of authority because they were found to be more sagacious than even the wisest men in King Nebuchadnezzar's kingdom. It all started when the king had a dream that neither he nor his wise men could interpret. Daniel was called before the king to interpret the dream. However, Daniel took the matter to God, and God gave him the interpretation, which Daniel shared with Nebuchadnezzar. The king was so pleased that he glorified God and promoted Daniel, Shadrach, Meshach, and Abednego. The same king who promoted the young men later wanted them thrown in the fiery furnace. Although these young men held prominent positions, they were about to face a life-or-death situation.

Nebuchadnezzar commissioned his image in gold, and at the dedication commanded that at the sound of music everyone had to bow down and worship the golden image. Well, as you can imagine, everyone did bow down, except for the three Jews, Shadrach, Meshach, and Abednego. Because they didn't bow, Nebuchadnezzar was angry and commanded that they be thrown in the burning, fiery furnace. The king was so angry with the boys that he requested for the furnace to be heated up seven times hotter than normal.

Why? Because there was something in them the enemy wanted to burn up. You must realize your worth. The rest of the crowd wasn't worth burning up. I think it's important for me to share with you that it's estimated there were at least 300,000 in attendance that day. However, only three stood for something, and the rest bowed for nothing. The next time your enemy comes after you, just tell yourself there has to be something very valuable inside you for the enemy to come after you over and over again. Remember–everyone else bowed except three men. This is a clear indication that some of us are carrying around something very valuable to the Kingdom. This also let me know that their worth was at least seven times greater than the other men.

Daniel 3:23-27 says:

"And these three men, Shadrach, Meshach, and Abednego, fell down bound into the midst of the burning fiery furnace. Then Nebuchadnezzar the king was astonished, and rose up in haste, and spake, and said unto his counsellors, Did not we cast three men bound into the midst of the fire? They answered and said unto the king, True, O king. He answered and said, Lo, I see four men loose, walking in the midst of the fire, and they have no hurt; and the form of the fourth is like the Son of God. Then Nebuchadnezzar came near to the mouth of the burning fiery furnace, and spake, and said, Shadrach, Meshach, and Abednego, ye servants of the most high God, come forth, and come hither. Then Shadrach, Meshach, and Abednego, came forth of the midst of the fire. And the princes, governors, and captains, and the king's counsellors, being gathered together, saw these men, upon whose bodies the fire had no power, nor was an hair of their head singed, neither were their coats changed, nor the smell of fire had passed on them."

I pray that this is a word for someone reading this book right now. I don't know your current condition or your present position, but I want to pause and let you know that no matter what you've done in life, as long as you are still breathing, you can repent right now and trust that God won't let you look like what you've been through.

I'm pretty sure that I don't look like the little boy who had a shoestring in his pants for a belt or had so-called nappy hair and grease all over his face. I'm pretty sure Tyler Perry doesn't look like he was abused or homeless. I'm pretty sure Michael Oher, Ravens offensive tackle, doesn't look like he was homeless or lived in foster care. I'm pretty sure Steve Harvey doesn't look like he was ever homeless or slept in his car. I'm pretty sure Lil' Kim doesn't look like she was kicked out of her house as a teenager and finding herself living on the streets. I'm pretty sure Oprah Winfrey doesn't look like she was abused. I'm pretty sure Kirk Franklin doesn't look like he grew up poor. I'm pretty sure Jennifer Lopez doesn't look like she slept on the sofa of her dance studio. I'm pretty sure comedian Jim Carrey doesn't look like he dropped out of high school and lived in a VW bus with his family parked in different places throughout Canada. I'm pretty sure Oscar winner Halle Berry doesn't look like she once stayed in a homeless shelter in her early 20s. I'm pretty sure Dr. Phil McGraw doesn't look like he was homeless at 12 years old and living in a car in Kansas City with his father.

If my story isn't convincing, I hope these people give you a glimpse of hope and inspire you to keep it moving. None of these people from what I've read and heard them say had an easy road. Even a little bit of success costs a lot. You must be willing to put in the work. Forget about your past and let's get going.

Chapter 4:

IT WASN'T MEANT TO MAKE YOU BITTER, BUT TO MAKE YOU BETTER

"And lest I should be exalted above measure through the abundance of the revelations, there was given to me a thorn in the flesh, the messenger of Satan to buffet me, lest I should be exalted above measure."
2 Corinthians 12:7

As life would have it, you'd be amazed by the bitter people that are walking around every single day, just bitter...
- bitter because of how they were raised.
- bitter about what happened twenty years ago.
- bitter because their father wasn't there.
- bitter because their mother didn't support them.
- bitter because they didn't make the cheer

team and someone less qualified did.
• bitter at their teacher.
• bitter at the preacher.
• bitter because things are not like they planned at this point in their lives.
• bitter waking up.
• bitter lying down.
• bitter about their salary.
• bitter because someone makes more money than them.
• Just BITTER!

All the while, God allows what He plans to use to make you better to be a part of your affliction. You do remember that the righteous afflictions are many, right? I know we've all been taught that prayer changes things. I know we've been taught to pray about everything. I know we've been taught to ask, and it shall be done. However, I'm not sure how much emphasis has been put on praying in the will of God. Our prayer should always be, "If it's your will, Lord..." God will not always do what we ask because He's a sovereign God. He's not a man who's here to satisfy our fleshly desires only. He will answer the prayers that line up with His Word and His will. Who better could give us a lesson on how to come out better rather than bitter? In this chapter, we'll gain insight on how to better understand that everything isn't about us feeling good but about what's good for our Father. Ultimately, God is always trying to get us to be more like Him. Sometimes it's a painful process, but well worth it.

Paul sheds a bit of light on the nature of the trial he endured basically by using two words: "thorn" and "buffet". His thorn was in his flesh. It affected his physical man. The truth is that no one really knows what the thorn was. All we know for sure is that his thorn made preaching and ministering to the churches a challenge for him.

Paul mentioned the persistence of his pain. He used the word "buffet". This means whatever his thorn was, it continually bothered him. He lived with it daily. While I don't know what it was, I do know it was used to keep him humble, and he prayed and asked God to remove it three times. God did not remove it because He was using Paul and the thorn for his good.

This backs up what I mentioned earlier regarding our prayers. No, God doesn't always return what we ask with the answer we expect. However, just because we don't see immediate results, it does not mean that God didn't answer.

We must trust that our God always knows what's best for us. Paul's buffet came to him from being "exalted above measure", which simply means, "to keep one from lifting himself above one's place". Understandably, Paul had received plenty of blessings and favor, and it seemed to concern God that he might begin to think of himself too highly. He had been used by God mightily.

Like Paul, we have to be very careful when God blesses us or decides to use us in ways that He's not using others. I think it's very easy for us to get high-minded. As a pastor, I've seen it a number of times among preachers and pastors. For whatever reason, many pastors measure success by how many members are in your congregation. I can't count how many times I've been asked the question, "Hey, doc, how many members you got?", especially among the African American Baptist pastors. I really want to tell them, "We don't have any." That's another book.

The church is God's bride. It's really sad, but many of the brothers don't want to fellowship with you if your membership isn't competitive to theirs in size and numbers. So sad. Maybe this is what God was trying to prevent Paul from. I know how dangerous it can be, and I know God will remove any of us if we get lifted up or he'll allow a thorn to come and buffet us.

I'm not sure how much you know about thorns, but growing up in the country, you get to see a variety of trees, including thorn trees. The point or tip of a thorn is as sharp as a needle. Yes, I've been stuck by one a time or two or three. I think it's really important for us to understand that the thorns in our lives may have been carried out by Satan, but they were conceived by our God. With that in mind, whatever thorn afflicts us is part of God's plan. No, He's never out to hurt us. Unfortunately, sometimes what helps us the most happens to hurt the worst. However, I'm here to tell you God's intention is never to take you out but rather to bring you out.

He wants us to become more and more like Him each day, so whatever your thorn is, don't allow it to make you bitter. Tell yourself, "I'm going to be better after this." I believe it was David who said, "It was good for me that I was afflicted." We must be the same way. All he was saying is God knew he was on the wrong path and permitted a thorn to buffet him so that he could get back in line with God's Word.

Again, don't be angry with the way God decides to keep you from destroying yourself. Learn how to say, "Thank you, Lord, that you love and care enough about me that you help me even when I don't realize I need help." After all, who else can look ahead of time and give us what we need to assure that we finish our course?

I know we've talked a bit about Paul, and you've had an opportunity to peek into my past. Now, as scripture records, let a man examine himself. I think in doing so, we'll better understand the purpose of our buffeting.

The Word of God says in Jeremiah 29:11 (NIV), "For I know the plans I have for you...plans to give you hope and a future."

It isn't God's plan, will, or desire that we suffer except if it brings us to submission or brings Him glory. The one thing you can't miss is that our primary duty is to bring our Heavenly Father glory. Therefore, He will continue to use whatever method He decides to use to get us to the place He wants us to be. Sometimes that means being incarcerated for long periods of time. This does not mean we have the right to blame God for our own behavior that lands us behind bars. God just has a way of using our time in lockdown to mold and shape us to be vessels that He can use. Unfortunately, some people have to stay longer than others to learn their lessons. There are other times people find themselves back behind bars time and time again. Yes, God loves you, but He'll let you go behind bars as many times as it takes to get you to the place He wants you.

I am not saying this is the only way God teaches us. I know that jails are crowded all across the country with people who thought they were slick enough to do the crime without doing any time. This is one of the motivating factors for me to write this book. I want to let men especially know that they are worth way more than any jail has to offer. As an African American brother, my heart is saddened every day I turn the television, computer, or even cell phone on and see us shooting each other. We kill each other so often, senselessly, until it seems the white men, particularly white policemen, feel they are justified in shooting us.

I want every man, every son, every brother, every nephew, every father, every uncle, and every grandfather to know there's an "A" in every man. I really want us to take a moment to realize there's worth in all of us. No matter what you've done, there's nothing that God won't forgive you for. You just have to be for real when you confess, acknowledge, and repent. Our God is willing, waiting, and ready to wash you whiter than snow. Seems impossible, huh? He's the only one who can do it. You have too much left inside of you to walk around bitter every day of your life. I'm not sure if this helps, but there's not one of us who hasn't experienced heartbreaks and troubled times. We all have a list of things we could be bitter about. We have made the choice to use our troubles and heartaches to make us better.

I must be honest, and I believe others can attest, that it wasn't our sunshiny days that drew us closer to God. It was those dark, difficult days that caused us to yearn for the love and closeness of God. It's in the valley we grow, not on the mountaintop. I really want to encourage you not to waste your valley experience.

I was told a story once about an old, mean-spirited lady who nearly went out of her way to treat her neighbor badly. Both of the women lived in the country. The mean-spirited lady took care of her husband's cows every day. They had a fenced in backyard where she kept her favorite cow. Being mean, she would scoop the cow manure up every day and throw it in her neighbor's yard. Just bitter! She did this for several weeks. The neighbor never said anything to her; she would just spread the manure all over her yard every day that the mean lady threw it across the fence.

As it's been said, time brings about a change. One day, the sweet neighbor noticed her mean neighbor hadn't thrown any manure in her yard in a couple of weeks. Although she had more than enough already, being the nice Christian woman that she was, she decided to go next door and check on the lady. Lo and behold, her health was failing rapidly. She was no longer able to walk without assistance. The sweet lady would go over and assist "Meany" every day. She felt it was her Christian duty. After all, no one else came to see her.

One day, she asked the lady if she would like to take a walk outside. She knew the lady enjoyed the outdoors because she would come outside and throw manure in her yard every day.

"Sure," she replied. She assisted the lady as they slowly walked out on her back porch.

The lady seemed to have gained strength out of nowhere and asked her Christian neighbor, "Oh my, where in the world did you get all of those beautiful red roses? I've never seen such beautiful roses in all my days. Your yard is covered with roses."

The Christian lady said with a gentle smile, "I planted some roses several weeks ago. They were barely growing, but when you threw your cow manure over into my yard, I spread it and used it for fertilizer, and my roses started growing all over my yard. Thanks! If it hadn't been for you, they all probably would have died."

You see, you've got to learn how to use what was meant to harm you to help you. Scriptures teach us that there are no weapon formed against us that will prosper. Too many of us get upset over the forming. Let your enemies plot and plan all they want. God knows the plans He has for you– to prosper you and not harm you.

Don't waste another minute being upset, angry, or frustrated about what happened to you. Don't even waste another minute thinking about who snitched on you or ratted you out. I encourage you to let today be the beginning of the best days of the rest of your life. They may be laughing now, but they'll be looking and lusting later. Eyes haven't seen, ears haven't heard, and neither has it entered in your heart how great the things God has in store for you will be.

I encourage you to say "Goodbye, Bitter!" and "Hello, Better!"

Chapter 5:

HOW TO BOUNCE BACK
FROM A SETBACK

"There was a man in the land of Uz, whose name was Job; and that man was perfect and upright, and one that feared God, and eschewed evil. And there were born unto him seven sons and three daughters. His substance also was seven thousand sheep, and three thousand camels, and five hundred yoke of oxen, and five hundred she asses, and a very great household; so that this man was the greatest of all the men of the east."
Job 1:1-3

One of the greatest challenges for any man is to bounce back from a setback. Guilt, shame, the enemy, foes, lack of confidence, and lack of forgiveness of self can deter us, just to name a few. It's a long, lonely road trying to get back up again. However, we must do like Job. Even when we complain, we must continue trusting God and not let anything or anyone persuade us to do or say anything that does not line up with the Word of God. That's why it is so important to do as Paul instructed Timothy to do– study God's Word.

I want to be totally open and honest with you. We shouldn't wait until we're down and out or until we are on lockdown or even until the storms of life are raging in our lives. We should obey scripture and meditate on God's Word daily.

It is definitely clear to me that Job knew something about the goodness and faithfulness of God. Job did not allow the loss of his family, friends, foes, finances, or future to change his faith. Yes, he got upset with God and wished he were dead. As a matter of fact, he regretted even being born. But he somehow still maintained his integrity.

I trust that when we look into the life of Job, we can walk away with a broader understanding that man truly was born of a woman of a few days and those days were filled with trouble. Job even acknowledges that he came into the world naked, and he would leave the world naked. In other words, Job is saying that he brought nothing into this world, and he expected to carry nothing with him out of this world.

I don't want you to confuse the word "perfect" in Job chapter one with the definition of "perfect" in the English dictionary. In the Word of God, "perfect" means that Job was blameless and upright, feared God with reverence, and abstained from and turned away from evil because he honored God.

Likewise, we should honor God with our lives as well as our bodies.

I have always believed that when we don't follow instructions, we're headed for destruction.

As you read about the life of Job, I'm sure you'll walk away wondering, How did this brother who was perfect and upright, feared God, and turned away from evil find himself in the midst of destruction?

Although it looks like it, this was never really about Job.

Notice what scripture says:

"And the Lord said unto Satan, Whence comest thou? Then Satan answered the Lord, and said, From going to and fro in the earth, and from walking up and down in it. And the Lord said unto Satan, Hast thou considered my servant Job, that there is none like him in the earth, a perfect and an upright man, one that feareth God, and escheweth evil?" (Job 1:7-8)

This was a perfect opportunity for God to show Satan, Job's friends, and all who would ever read the book of Job that He is omnipotent. He has the power to do anything He desires.

God was allowing Satan to have his way with Job because of nothing he had done. Even though that's exactly what his friends thought. When you become a child of God, you too will experience many afflictions that will not have anything to do with the right or wrong you've done in life, but instead act as a perfect way for God to receive glory.

Job fits the scripture that says many are the afflictions of the righteous but God delivers us from them all. No man who accepts Jesus as their Savior is exempted from the troubles, trials and tribulations of this life.

I don't know where you are in life at this very moment, but I want to let you know that God does. Even though there will be times you'll feel somewhat like Job, God's Word is still true. He'll never leave us or forsake us. I must forewarn you: He won't always pop up and do what we ask at the moment we feel like we're dying, but as a great songwriter says, He's a God you can't hurry, but He'll be there, don't worry.

Of course, it was a challenging time in Job's life. The Bible lets us know that in spite of Job being perfect and upright, trouble found his address, as it will mine and yours. The Bible tells us that Job had seven sons and three daughters. He had seven thousand sheep, three thousand camels, five hundred yoke of oxen, five hundred she asses (donkeys), and a very great household. This man was the greatest of all men of the east. Wow, this brother was truly blessed.

Here's what happened: one day, while Job's sons and daughters were at their oldest brother's house, a messenger came and told Job that his oxen were plowing while the asses (donkeys) were feeding beside them and the Sabeans (terrorizing robbers from Southwest Arabia) attacked and swooped down on them and took away the animals. They also killed the servants with "the edge of the sword", and "the fire of God" (lightning) fell from the heavens and burned up the sheep and the servants and consumed them. Also, the Chaldeans (marauding nomads from the Arabian desert) formed three bands and performed a raid on the camels and took them away and killed the servants with "the edge of the sword". As if that weren't enough, Job's sons and daughters were eating and drinking wine in their oldest brother's house, and suddenly, a great wind came from across the desert, struck the four corners of the house, fell on the young people, and killed all of them.

Now that you have the gist of the story, be careful when you say, "I feel just like Job." I'm sure all of us have dealt with some difficult times. However, I haven't met anyone personally who has experienced all of the tragedies Job did. I definitely haven't met anyone who maintained their integrity after such a loss.

I am not, in any way, minimizing the pain of others just because they didn't have the same experience as Job. There's a great lesson for us all in the life of Job. Job teaches us to keep our faith in God even when we face what seems to be a hopeless situation. One of the ways to do that is by remembering that the earth and the fullness thereof, the world and they who dwell therein, all belong to God. We brought nothing into this world, and we surely won't take anything with us when we leave.

Even our children belong to God.

Yes, our moms carried us until the days they birthed us, but it's good to know that it's all the amazing work of God. We live, move, and have our being because of who He is. If Job could go through what he went through and still not charge God foolishly, surely we can do the same. I like to believe that if God brings us to it, He'll bring us through it. I am not saying that everything we go through is something that God brings us to. We have to be honest that many, if not most, of our troubles have come from us being disobedient to the Word and will of God.

We can't go through life blaming everybody else for all of our failures. Yes, I'll admit, a lot of who we are can be contributed to our up-bringing. If we've never seen or lived in the house to witness a godly marriage, how can we have them? If we weren't raised in homes with working fathers, how would we know how to be godly providers? If we weren't raised in Christian homes, how do we know how to have one? I could go on and on, but I think you get my point.

While everything I just said or asked is true, there must be a degree of accountability accepted by every man. There comes a time in all of our lives that we must step up and take full responsibility for all of our actions. It can't always be blamed on the devil or anyone else.

I was only two years old when my parents separated (according to my sisters). According to them, my mom and dad had a really bad encounter– or should I say, a misunderstanding– and decided that it was best for them to live in separate homes. That's exactly what they did. They never divorced; thus, they never remarried. As strange as it may sound, they never lived far from each other. By the time I was old enough to know anything, I wasn't allowed to ask anything. In those days, you were always told to stay in a child's place. That meant you didn't ask grown folks about certain things. Well, that was fine with me because I had my mom and I had my dad. So, to be honest, nothing else really mattered. I would stay with my dad at night and hang with him on the weekends and then stay with my mom through the week during school days. I really couldn't tell they weren't still married because Dad would always be cutting Mom's hedges or they would be on the porch talking. On holidays, Dad would oftentimes be at Mom's house, sitting at the head of the table. So, it was all good with me.

The point of me sharing this with you is to eradicate all excuses for that person who says, "I was always in trouble and made bad decisions because I wasn't raised in a two-parent home." Neither was I. Again, we have to step up and be accountable for our actions. A person in denial can't be delivered.

If you noticed, Job's friends tried to blame him for all that happened to him, but Job never blamed God for what happened to him. He kept trusting and believing, even when the woman closest to him, his wife, tried to get him to curse God and die. You can't allow anybody to corrupt your belief in God. I don't care what things look like at this point in your life– keep trusting and holding on.

In chapter 1 and 2, Job loses everything he has. Thank God that wasn't the end of his story because God gives him double for his trouble in chapter 42. While "double for his trouble" sounds good, he really was blessed abundantly for his faith and obedience. In chapter 42 of Job, we find that the Lord sees Job praying for his friends during his captivity, and the Lord gives him twice as much as he had before. Notice that Job prays for his friends. Even if out of obligation, it is still very significant. So many ministers overlook this when preaching or speaking. When you don't exegete this appropriately, it makes it look like Job does not receive double for his trouble. Yes, he receives double, but I suggest it is for his obedience and not necessarily for his trouble. After all, God didn't owe Job anything.

Job did something many of us would never consider doing. Job prayed for the same people who told him his sin was the reason he was suffering. This is a valuable lesson. We must learn to forgive and pray for the wellbeing of others, no matter what they have said about us or done to us. The Bible teaches us to love our enemies, bless those who curse us, do good to those who hate us, and pray for those who despitefully use us and even persecute us. This is how to bounce back from a terrible setback. You might not be rewarded the same way Job was, but your faithfulness and obedience won't go unnoticed by God.

The world teaches us not to be cowards and do the same to others as they do to us. In other words, the message is "an eye for an eye". But that's not God's way. I can promise you if you obey God, forgive others, and pray for others (including your enemies), God will bless you richly. All of His blessings don't necessarily come in financial form. He has so many other ways to bless you.

It's time to bounce back.

Let go of any unforgiveness, any hatred, any malice, any jealousy– anything that stands between you and God. You can get way more from God praying than you'll ever receive pouting.

Chapter 6:

WHEN YOU'RE DOWN TO NOTHING GOD IS UP TO SOMETHING

"And when he came to himself, he said,
how many hired servants of my father's
have bread enough and to spare,
and I perish with hunger!"
Luke 15:17

Perhaps all of us have been in a "down to nothing" position similar to the one the younger of two sons in the scripture above is in. Amazingly and oftentimes devastatingly, this is where we will end up when we follow our own GPS.

Here is a young man who had it made at home with a father who had plenty. He made the same mistake as so many of us have made, thinking the grass is greener on the other side, only to get to the other side and realize the grass was actually brown and dried up and that the owner had a green bulb shining on his dry grass.

In the scripture, this brother is sitting around the house one day and gets up enough nerve to ask his father to give him whatever he has in his will to give him later. Of course, this request is very disrespectful, but his father decides to honor his request and divide his assets with his younger son. As life would have it, this brother is in for a rude awakening. When his money gets funny, so do his so-called friends. He takes seven drastic steps downward, and thanks be to God that He left the door open for him to take seven steps upwards.

Downward Steps

Step One– Self-Will: The younger son said to his father, "Give me the portion of goods that falleth to me" (Luke 15:12). In those days, a father could either grant inheritance before or after his death, but it was usually done after. The younger son asks for a special exception, motivated by foolishness and greed. He has no one to blame for whatever the outcome is but himself.

Step Two– Selfishness: It's clear he's thinking only of himself. He doesn't take into consideration how it could makes his father feel. He's looking to feel good and have a good time right away at any expense. I'm sure he had been thinking this over for a long time.

This is the same position so many of us take, whether we're robbers, murderers, dope dealers, liars, cheaters, gamblers, alcoholics, drug addicts, or any manner of selfish people who project harm onto others while satisfying our flesh temporarily. Many have destroyed in thirty minutes what it took years to build, not counting the cost.

Step Three– Separation: He takes his journey into a faraway country. This brother decides to go a long way from home. That's just like the devil. He wants to take us far away from Jesus. His goal is to get us as far away as possible and as deep into sin as he can before he leaves. Keep in mind that Jesus indicates in John 10:10 that Satan comes to kill, steal, and destroy.

Step Four– Sensuality: The son wastes his inheritance and foregoes righteous living. He leaves the area to become independent of his father and lives a prodigal (reckless, foolish, extravagant) life. No doubt it was fun while it lasted. We have to be very careful separating ourselves from those who genuinely love us just to connect with those who only love what we have.

Step Five– Spiritual Destitution: "And when he had spent all, there arose a mighty famine in that land; and he began to be in want" Luke 15:14. The son is completely to blame for the wasteful, foolish living and spending. He is not to blame for the severe famine but is afflicted by it nevertheless.

Step Six– Self-Abasement: "...he joined himself to one of the citizens of that country; and he sent him into his fields to feed swine" Luke 15:15. Driven by hunger and need, the son accepts work that was unacceptable and offensive to any righteous Jewish person during that time because swine were unclean under the law (Leviticus 11:7).

Step Seven– Starvation: No one gives him anything. The misery of the prodigal son should be a lesson to us all.

What a mighty God we serve. Even though we are to blame for most of the things that happens to us, our God still has His arms wide open, ready, and willing for us to return.

Upward Steps

Step One– Realization: The son comes to himself. In his misery, the prodigal son is finally able to think clearly. In his rebellion and disobedience, he wasn't himself. In his years of rioting, he was not himself. The prodigal version of him was not the real man. The real man was the penitent, not the prodigal. In his clear thinking, he doesn't think of how to improve conditions in the pigpen.

He doesn't blame his father, his brother, his friends, his boss, or the pigs. He recognizes his misery without focusing on it and instead focuses on his father. This brother is just like so many of us. He allowed an evil spirit to take over his mind and begin to do what he thought was right in his wrong mind. Therefore, what was actually wrong looked like it was the right thing to do. Thanks to God that He didn't give up on the young man and neither has God given up on you. You just need to come to yourself and realize it was you who made the mistake or the bad decision and stop blaming everyone else. The sooner you realize this, the sooner you can make your way back to your Father.

Step Two– Resolution: "I will arise and go to my father..." (Luke 15:18). Jesus doesn't say that the man thinks of his village or his home, but of his father. When the son returns to the father, he also comes back to the village and to the house, but his focus is on returning to his father. That is how we need to come back to God. Come back to Him first and foremost before coming back to church or friends or a relationship, and so on.

Step Three– Repentance: This brother in our reading repents by acknowledging his fault. He clearly states, "...I have sinned against heaven, and in thy sight..." (Luke 15:21). In his prepared speech to his father, the son shows his complete sense of unworthiness and an honest confession of sin. He does not even ask to be treated as a son, but as a hired servant. When it comes to repentance, saying "I'm sorry" isn't true repentance. God wants you to be apologetic enough to change your behavior.

"I have sinned against heaven, and in thy sight" shows a complete change of thinking. He didn't think like this before; now he makes no attempt to justify or excuse his sin. Likewise, we must admit and accept our faults.

The lost son demonstrates the repentance Jesus specifically spoke of in the previous parables of the lost sheep and the lost coin in this same chapter. After his misery, he thinks completely differently about his father, himself, and his home. The son asks for two things: First, "Father, give me", and then, "Father, make me." Only the second request brought joy.

Step Four– Return: "And he arose and came to his father..." (Luke 15:20). The prodigal first thinks, but he doesn't stop thinking. He doesn't just feel sorry and think about repenting – he actually does it. Merely thinking about a thing does not accomplish anything. May you, by divine grace, be turned from thinking to believing, or else your thoughts will only be thoughts. This is a clear picture that our Father is willing to let us return if we're willing to turn.

Step Five– Reconciliation: When the young man is yet a great way off, his father sees him, has compassion, runs, falls on his neck, and kisses him. "And the son said unto him, Father,

I have sinned against heaven, and in thy sight, and am no more worthy to be called thy son" (Luke 15:21). The father's love waited and never forgot. It was a love that fully received, not putting the son on probation. This was especially remarkable because the son had disgraced the family by his prodigal living. The depth of the son's repentance is matched only by the depth of the father's love. Likewise, our heavenly father is waiting on us all day every day. It doesn't matter what you did, when you did it, or how long ago it was. Our father is still waiting on us to repent and return to him, so wherever you are right now, get up and head back to your Father's house.

Step Six– Re-Clothing: The father tells the servants to bring forth the best robe and put it on him, put a ring on his hand, and shoes on his feet. Notice that none of the four things brought to the repentant prodigal are necessities; they are all meant to honor the son and make him know he is loved. The father does much more than merely meet his son's needs. That's the way our Heavenly Father wants to be with us. He doesn't want to withhold anything from us. However, there are certain things we can't have until we're prepared to handle them. All of these gifts for the son were at the house before he left. Sometimes in life, it takes us sitting in the hog pen to realize that we had everything all along.

Step Seven– Rejoicing: The father tells the servants to bring the fatted calf, kill it, eat, and be merry. They have a wonderful party with special clothing, jewelry, and food. It isn't just a situation of finding a lost son; it's as if he were back from the dead. That's exactly what our Father wants to do for us. He's waiting to celebrate with us when we come to Him or when we return to Him.

Chapter 7:
Your Present Place Doesn't Have to Be Your Permanent Place

"And they took him, and cast him into a pit:
and the pit was empty, there was no water in it."
Genesis 37:24

This is a story of a seventeen-year-old boy who really experienced a bittersweet life. This brother was loved and hated, favored and abused, tempted and trusted, exalted and abased. However, at no point in the 110 years of Joseph's life did he ever seem to take his eyes off God or cease to trust Him. Adversity didn't harden his character and prosperity didn't ruin him. Joseph was the same in private as he was in public. He was the real thing. He was truly a man of God.

As I examine the life of Joseph, I am definitely intrigued and fascinated by his integrity. After all, it's challenging to read the story of Joseph's life and not see a man committed to God. His brothers not only stripped him out of his coat, but they in fact stripped him down to nothing– or so they thought.

Don't miss it.

They thought they had taken what was most important to him when they took his coat, but clearly the coat was more important to them than it was to him. When you read the backdrop of Joseph's life, you'll find out that his brothers– yes, I said his biological brothers– betrayed him and sold him as a slave. They sold him to some Ishmaelite merchant for less than a hundred dollars. I know it's hard to believe this really did happen, but it actually did. They took him to Egypt and put him up for sale in that land.

Imagine with me for a moment that you are seventeen years old, you were your father's favored son out of twelve sons, and your father had chosen you to be the head of the family and given you a beautiful robe to symbolize the fact that you were in charge. I mean, after all, you are on a path to power, influence, and prominence in your family. Then, in the blink of an eye, you are stripped of the very coat that signified who you were.

You are stripped of your coat, and you are betrayed by people who should have loved, supported, and been happy for you. You are separated from your father, the one who's responsible for setting you on the path of prominence. You are sold as a slave, carried off into a strange land, and auctioned off as a slave. My question is: could you have gone through all of this and maintained your integrity and faithfulness to God?

Once you read the entire story concerning the life of Joseph, you'll soon discover he really didn't lose his coat – he left his coat. That's a word for somebody. You can't carry everything you used to have to your designed divine destination. So, don't ever let losing stuff cause you to get lost.

Just because you are going through trials, trouble, turbulence, and tribulation, it doesn't mean that God isn't working on your behalf. You might not see or feel His presence, but that doesn't mean that He isn't present. You have to know as a believer that all things are working for your good. So many things happened to Joseph, but watch what happened for Joseph. What Joseph's brothers didn't know was that it all was a setup for Joseph to be blessed.

Consider these points:
- Joseph wouldn't be in his elevated position later if he hadn't gone through his past problems.
- If his brothers hadn't beaten him down, he wouldn't have been in a position to be lifted up.

- If they didn't put him in the pit, he never would have been sold to Egypt.
- If he hadn't been sold to slavery in Egypt, he wouldn't have been working for Potiphar.
- If he hadn't been working for Potiphar, Potiphar's wife never would have lied on him.
- If Potiphar's wife never lied on him, he never would have gone to jail.
- If he never went to jail, he never would have met the cupbearer and the baker.
- If he never met the cupbearer and the baker, they wouldn't have told the king about him.
- If they never told the king about him, he never would have interpreted his dream.
- If he had never interpreted the dream, he never would have been promoted.
- If he were never promoted over agriculture, the world would have starved to death.

Therefore, learn to tell God thank you for every hill and valley He took you over and through to get you to your divine destination. Yes, it looked like Joseph was going to be in the pit of life forever, but God turned his situation around. God can turn what seems to be your worst day ever into your best day ever.

I know firsthand the depth of being down to nothing and thinking things for me would always be just what they were. I shared many of my struggles with you in chapter 2. Living on our family farm meant every time I walked out the front door, as far as I could see to the left, right, in front of me and behind me, there was nothing but woods and farmland for miles and miles. I'm the youngest of four boys and all three of my brothers and every other man in the community were all driving tractors to make a living.

Neither my mother nor my father had driver's licenses or a vehicle to drive. That meant we either walked everywhere we went or caught a ride. There was this man we called Mr. Peley (of course no one called him by his real name Mr. Perry Lee) who would always take a truckload to town each Saturday – for a small fee, of course. Mr. Perry Lee would park on the front street in town and let everybody know that he would be pulling off in exactly an hour and a half. He was very prompt. I recall guys running to jump on the back of the truck almost every Saturday as Mr. Peley made his way out of town. Trust me, if you weren't on the truck at the time Mr. Peley told you to be, you were bound to get left.

My point is that my parents didn't have any type of transportation. Mom or dad had to pay someone to take us everywhere we went, or we walked, and that I did countless times. I didn't really mind walking; I just hated when we would have on our nice clothes (or what we considered nice) walking up and down the roads and people with vehicles would come by driving so fast on the graveled road and dust us up.

I would always say, "One day when I grow up, I'm going to get me a car and I won't have to worry about walking or getting dust all over me anymore." Something on the inside would keep reminding me, "It won't always be like this." As I looked in old catalogs and books, it gave me hope that one day I would get one of those cars. I will never forget purchasing my first car. There was a used car lot back in the day, "Bud's Used Cars", on University Avenue here in Little Rock, Arkansas. A semi-heavyset white man owned the car lot. I had gone by the car lot on several occasions but never stopped because I didn't have any money. I would always look out the window each time I rode by with someone to see what was on the lot.

One day, I was out walking as I often did and decided to walk up University to see what was on the lot. I probably need to inform you that I had just moved to Little Rock from the country and landed a part time job making $3.40 an hour, averaging about 20 to 25 hours a week. Of course, taxes and child support came out first, which usually left me around $60 to $70 to bring home each week. Yes, I had to give whoever I was staying with a few dollars.

However, I thought I would go up to the car lot this particular day to browse the lot. As I walked around a few minutes, the slightly heavy-set white man came out and waited on me.

He asked, "Can I help you, young man?"

"No sir, not really," I replied. "I'm just looking around."

"I know that, but you're looking at cars."

"Yeah, but I'm not here to purchase one today," I said. "I'm just looking, so when I get my money together, I'll have an idea of what I can get and where I'll want to purchase it from."

He then asked me if I saw a car I wanted.

I chuckled and said, "Yes, if I had the money, I would probably get that rust-colored Buick.

"Oh, that 72 Buick Skylark?"

I said yes.

"That's a pretty good little car," he said. "It really needs a valve job, but other than that, it's a nice little car. I'll sell it to you like it is for $950, or I'll get the valve fixed and sell it to you for $1,200.

"If I was going to purchase it..." I said. "I would buy it just like it is and drive it to my hometown, Marvell, and let a guy I know fix it."

He couldn't resist the salesman's conviction that was on him.

He asked, "Would you like that car?"

"Yes," I said. "But I don't have the money today to purchase it.

"How much money do you have?"

"Aww, I don't have but forty dollars on me today."

Honestly, that's all I had period. He went inside, got the keys, and let me start it up and look inside.

Then he said, "Come on, let's go inside."

I followed him inside as he sat behind his desk, and I sat in a seat directly across from him.

"Let me have the forty dollars."

I somewhat stared him down the entire time I was sliding my hands in my pockets. I thought it was some kind of joke. No one can purchase a car worth anything with a $40 down payment. I gave him the $40, and he began to write me out a receipt.

He looked at me and said, "From now on, don't ever say what can't happen. Always remember an owner can do whatever he wants to with what belongs to him. Bring me $260 in two weeks. That'll be your $300 down payment, and your balance will be $650."

I left the car lot with the biggest smile in disbelief. I could not believe I had just put my first car on layaway with $40 down. Of course, this has been my life story for anyone who doubts what they can do.

Let's take a look at my car purchasing journey. I wanted to share this for the person who may look at what they're driving now without knowing what they rode in to get where you are. It's okay to start from the bottom, remembering that your present place doesn't have to be your permanent place. Success doesn't usually happen overnight but over time.

First car: 1972 Buick Skylark (rust)
Second car: 1971 Ford Mustang (green)
Third car: 1976 Oldsmobile Cutlass (cream/beige)
Fourth car: 1975 Ford Granada (red)
Fifth car: 1976 Camaro (blue)
Sixth car: 1982 Cutlass Supreme (gray)
Seventh car: Mitsubishi Eclipse (red)
Eighth car: 1982 Z 200 (gray)
Ninth car: 1997 Hyundai Excel (red)
Tenth car: 1992 Nissan Maxima (pearl)
Eleventh car: 1998 Mitsubishi eclipse (black)
Twelfth car: 2000 G20t Infiniti (white)
Thirteenth car: 1996 Mitsubishi pick up (red)
Fourteenth car: 2005 GS300 Lexus (silver)
Fifteenth car: 1998 Ford Ranger (black)
Sixteenth car: 2001 G20t Infiniti (gold)
Seventeenth car: 2001 Ford Ranger (white)
Eighteenth car: 2010 GX 470 Lexus (gold) (15 years old– I still drive it every day)
Nineteenth car: Um...let's just say I kind of like it...

A couple of the cars might be out of order as it relates to purchasing, but I owned them all at one time. Oh, I almost forgot to tell you about the 1975 Ford Granada I drove with a mustang engine in it. One Friday morning, as I was getting dressed for work, I heard my brothers-in-law from my first marriage arguing seemingly uncontrollably.

They argued so long that I stepped in and said to one of them, "Hey, man, you can drive my car today. Just drop me off at work and be back to pick me up at 3:30 pm."

3:30 came...4:00 came...4:30 rolled around... and no brother-in-law.

I made a phone call to their cousin who they spent a lot of time with, and the first thing he said was, "Man, dude didn't call you?"

I said, "No, what's up?"

"Dude wrecked your car and parked it behind the apartment off of 65th Street."

I asked him if he could come pick me up.

He said, "Yes, I'll be right there."

He picked me up from my job and took me straight to my car I had "just paid off". As we were riding, he said, the front end was totally damaged. Instead of going to work like he said he was, he went to work, picked up his check, and went and got some weed. Clearly, he was feeling so good that he pulled out in front of a vehicle. It damaged my vehicle but only left a mark on the bumper of the other vehicle.

Fast forward– I found a Ford Granada body and got a guy to take the motor out of my Mustang and put it in the Granada. Of course, it didn't fit properly. The motor was attached to only one motor mount. The other side of the motor was literally resting on the frame of the car. I had to get another guy to make a driveshaft that would be long enough. I got another guy to put in three transmissions from a junkyard until we got one that was working. I took the radiator from the Mustang, a 2x4, and a cloth hanger and tied the radiator down. I left that night with faith, a half pack of cigarettes, and less than $100, and drove all the way to Del Valley, Texas, with everything I owned in the vehicle. Nobody but God!

I mentioned this particular vehicle in detail to let you know that anything is possible. I want to make it known, while your present place may perhaps be dark and dismal, it doesn't have to be your permanent place. Things do not happen overnight, so don't give up. Keep in mind that when I left home a couple years after graduation, I left walking – as in, I owned no transportation. I caught a ride to Little Rock with my friend and stayed with him a while and bounced around until I got my own place. Once I moved from the country, I didn't return to live there. This does not indicate there's something wrong with living in the country. I'm just saying.

Chapter 8:

Don't Look Back

"But his wife looked back from behind him, and she became a pillar of salt."
Genesis 19:26

The Bible tells us that Lot was the nephew of Abraham. Following a quarrel, Abraham and Lot had to part, and Abraham let Lot choose the stretch of land he would settle on. Lot chose the best stretch, one that was close to the kingdom of Sodom. The kingdoms of Sodom and Gomorrah were situated just north of the Dead Sea, on the Jordan River plain, and known for their green, well-watered land. Unfortunately, they were also known as places of sin and wickedness.

Lot settled in the area, became a citizen of Sodom, and married a Sodomite woman. Later on, his daughters became engaged to men from Sodom. As a relative of Abraham, who had saved Sodom from the Elamite invasion during the Battle of Siddim, Lot was a highly respected member of the community and even became Sodom's mayor.

However, at some point, God became angry with the people of Sodom and decided to destroy the city, as not even ten righteous people could be found in all of it. Lot was the only righteous person in the city, so God had decided to spare him and his family. To warn him of what was about to happen, God sent two angels to Sodom. Lot invited them to stay with his family, and that night, Lot and his wife entertained them in their home.

The following morning, the angels hastened Lot and his family to leave the city before its destruction. As the family had a hard time leaving all the pleasures and luxuries of Sodom behind, the angels had to threaten them by saying they had to escape for their lives and could not look behind them or stay anywhere in the valley; they had to escape to the mountains or else they would be swept away.

As they were escaping, the sky rained brimstone and fire on Sodom. Lot's wife, perhaps feeling regret to be leaving Sodom behind and heading into the unknown, cast a last look behind her. But as she did so, vapors of sulfur overtook her, and she became a pillar of salt. Lot's wife was turned to a pillar of salt because she looked back behind after the angels had specifically warned not to look behind them (Genesis 19:17).

I was privileged enough to visit the pillar of salt known as "Lot's Wife" during my tour to the Dead Sea. If you ever visit Israel, you can actually go to Mount Sodom, a hill which lies at the southwestern part of the Dead Sea, and there you'll see it. It is so amazing – it stands at 220 meters high, 8 kilometers long, and 3 kilometers wide, is composed of 80 percent salt and is capped by a layer of clay, limestone, and conglomerate. However, due to weathering, some portions of the hill have gradually separated from it; one of them is the tall pillar "Lot's Wife".

I have in my possession a piece of the salt that I picked up during my visit to Mount Sodom. Not only is the pillar of Lot's wife there, but you'll notice she's still looking back at Sodom and Gomorrah.

One of the tricks of Satan is to get you to look back at your past with hopes of getting you to go back. Satan really wanted to kill you when you were back there, but God brought you out. So, now he's willing to spend the remainder of his life (which isn't much longer) and yours trying to get you to look back long enough to desire to go back. However, don't be fooled by that because if Satan can get you to go back where God has brought you from, he intends to kill and destroy you this time.

I don't know who this is speaking to, but don't go back and stop looking back. The Word teaches us to press forward. Whether it was bad and we won't forget or it was good and we don't want to forget it, Satan wants to keep reminding us of our past.

The good news is that Satan can't make you look back at your past or go back to your past. That decision is totally up to each individual. Yes, we make the decision to move forward. All of us wrestle with letting go of our past completely. Not all of our past was bad, but we are aiming for a brighter and more productive future.

Paul mentions leaving his past behind, saying:

"Brothers and sisters, I do not consider that I have made it my own yet; but one thing I do: forgetting what lies behind and reaching forward to what lies ahead, I press on toward the goal to win the [heavenly] prize of the upward call of God in Christ Jesus" (Philippians 3:13-14, AMP).

All of Paul's past experiences were not bad, but to obtain the prize he had his eyes focused on, he knew it was important to let go of his past. Paul was sagacious enough to know that his past successes could be a hindrance just like his past failures. Either way, he recommends forgetting our past.

I am well aware of the many issues that we all have to overcome. However, somehow and some way, we must keep it moving. You must realize that if you didn't have anything to offer, Satan wouldn't try so hard to derail you from your divine destination. Satan has peeked in on your future, and he knows you are a threat every morning your feet hit the floor. You've got to get this. The real fight is what's inside of you. Your greatness. We are not each other's real problem. The truth is, we don't wrestle against flesh and blood, but against principalities, against powers, against rulers of darkness, and against spiritual wickedness in high places.

There's an "A" in each of you. You're awesome. Think about it: Satan wouldn't waste his time on you if you weren't. Keep in mind that the devil is a distractor, deceiver, destroyer, demon, depressor and a "delusion-arian". Just outright devilish and devious.

We have to watch how we treat each other.

When one black brother kills another black brother senselessly, it seems as though police officers feel justified to shoot a brother:

• in his back while walking in the opposite direction.

• in his chest while his children are in the backseat watching and witnessing.

• in his own apartment while sitting on his

sofa eating ice cream.
- in his home while lying in bed.
- for walking in his own neighborhood.
- for having a water gun in his hand.
- for walking with a hood on his head.
- for having Skittles in his hand.
- for reaching for his driver's license.
- for jogging in his neighborhood.
- for selling CDs.
- for standing in his grandma's backyard using his cell phone.
- for selling cigarettes to another brother.
- for playing with a toy gun in the park.
- for walking with a friend in Ferguson.
- for being bipolar.
- for reaching inside his truck.

I think you get my point. So, yes, I understand how challenging it is not to look back when there seems to be so much to look back at. However, we must make the decision to learn from our past and reach for greatness in the future. My word for all men is don't give up, don't give in, and don't give out. I know it's been rough, especially in 2020, but better days are coming. Seasons come and go. I'm decreeing and declaring with you that this is your season.

Chapter 9:

PRAYER STILL WORKS

"And at midnight Paul and Silas prayed, and sang praises unto God: and the prisoners heard them. And suddenly there was a great earthquake, so that the foundations of the prison were shaken: and immediately all the doors were opened, and every one's bands were loosed."
Acts 16:25-26

In this chapter, I hope to shed some light on the best thing to do when you don't know what else to do. If you have never been there, as the saints of old would say, just keep living. Life challenges can get you down so bad that you don't even feel like praying. Even when you get to this point, God knows your thoughts, and the Holy Spirit will tell Him everything that's in your heart. Never feel like you're the only one who has been in that place.

Paul and Silas found themselves in prison through no fault on their own. They were in prison for doing the work of Christ.

Here's a little background regarding why Paul and Silas were in jail, found in Acts 16:16-40:

There was a certain damsel or slave girl who had a spirit of divination (that is, a demonic spirit claiming to foretell the future and discover hidden knowledge), and she brought her owners a good profit by fortune-telling. She followed after Paul and Silas and kept screaming and shouting, "These men are servants of the Most High God! They are proclaiming to you the way of salvation!" She continued doing this for several days. Then Paul, being greatly annoyed and worn out, turned and said to the spirit inside her, "I command you in the name of Jesus Christ (as His representative) to come out of her!" And it came out at that very moment. But when her owners saw that their hope of profit was gone, they seized Paul and Silas and dragged them before the authorities in the marketplace (where trials were held). When they brought them before the chief magistrates, they said, "These men, who are Jews, are throwing our city into confusion and causing trouble. They are publicly teaching customs which are unlawful for us, as Romans, to accept or observe." The crowd also joined in the attack against them, and the chief magistrates tore their robes off them and ordered that Paul and Silas be beaten with rods. After striking them many times (with the rods), they threw them into prison, commanding the jailer to guard them securely. He, having received such a strict command, threw them into the inner prison (dungeon) and fastened their feet in the stocks (in an agonizing position). But at about midnight, when Paul and Silas were praying and singing hymns of praise to God, and the prisoners were listening to them, suddenly there was a great earthquake, so powerful that the very foundations of the prison were shaken, and at once all the doors were opened and everyone's chains were unfastened. When the jailer, shaken out of sleep, saw the prison doors open, he drew his sword and was about to kill himself, thinking that the prisoners had escaped. But Paul shouted, "Do not hurt yourself, we are all here!" Then the jailer called for torches and rushed in, and he fell down before Paul and Silas, trembling with fear. After he brought them out of the inner prison, he said, "Sirs, what must I do to be saved?" And they answered, "Believe in the Lord Jesus as your personal Savior and entrust yourself to Him, and you will be saved, you and your household (if they also believe)." And they spoke the Word of the Lord concerning eternal salvation through faith in Christ to him and to all who were in his house. And he took them that very hour of the night, washed their bloody wounds, and immediately he was baptized – he and all his household. Then he brought them into his house, set food before them, and rejoiced greatly since he had believed in God with his entire family, accepting with joy what had been made known to them about the Christ. Now when the day came, the chief magistrates sent their officers, saying, "Release those men." And the jailer repeated the words to Paul, saying, "The chief magistrates have sent word to release you, so come out now and go in peace." But Paul said to them, "They have beaten us in public without a trial, men who are Romans, and have thrown us into prison; and now they are sending us out secretly? No! Let them come here themselves and bring us out!" The officers reported this message to the chief magistrates, and when they heard that the prisoners were Romans, they were frightened, so they came to the prison and appealed to them with apologies, and when they brought them out, they kept begging them to leave the city. So, they left the prison and went to Lydia's house, and when they had seen the brothers and sisters, they encouraged and comforted them, and then left.

Here's what's interesting: when the woman is no longer able to bring her master's profit, they arrest Paul and Silas by dragging them into the marketplace before the authorities.

Check this out: Paul and Silas are singled out. Luke and Timothy are still with them at this point. I'm sure they let them get by because Luke was a gentile and Timothy was half Jewish. There you have it; prayer still works! Yes, we the children of God have to face many challenges because of our love, the Lord Jesus Christ. Being a child of God does not exempt us from being thrown in prison, thrown in the lion's den, thrown in the pit, thrown in the fiery furnace, being lied on, being talked about, or any other evil thing you can think of. Yes, many are the afflictions of the righteous, but God will deliver us from them all. While God might not stop our enemy from throwing us in the "lion's den", He definitely will not let him have his way with us. You can always count on God. If He doesn't stop your enemy from throwing you in the den, it's likely that He plans to get in with you. Honestly, I'd rather be in a lion's den with God than be outside of the den without God.

There are so many instances throughout the Word of God that show us that God is a promise keeper. Here's the good news– God has assured us that if we do lose our lives for Him, He will give them back to us. So, yes, prayer still works, even if it doesn't work the way we think it should.

Many people think prayer is a "to-do list" for God because scripture says to ask what you will and it shall be done unto you. Make your request known. Two can join together and ask what they will. These scriptures are true, but we must pray within the will of God. We can't ever allow our prayer to suggest for God to come out of His will. The Bible calls this "praying amiss". Praying vain words.

We must also keep in mind when we are facing challenges in our lives that our ultimate goal as children of God is to bring God glory with our lives, which means that there will be many times we'll have to turn our cheek or experience things we have no desire to experience for the sake of Christ.

Praying doesn't mean that we won't go through things or that God will come running at our every beck and call. It's our way of communicating with God. We can't just lay a "to-do list" before God on our way out the door and pick it back up when we return to see what all God has done on our list. Prayer is a two-way street. When we pray, we must wait for God to speak to us, not just answer what we ask.

As my dad before he went to be with the Lord would always sing, you can't hurry God.

Chapter 10:

WHERE DO I GO FROM HERE?

"And I will restore to you the years that the locust hath eaten, the cankerworm, and the caterpillar, and the palmerworm, my great army which I sent among you."
Joel 2:25

This could be the most important chapter in the entire book. If you don't make a conscious decision that you're ready to get to your divine destination, then this will be just another book you've read and put in your library. Let me go ahead and share with you now. The utopia that most people are chasing does not exist. It's like chasing the pot of gold at the end of the rainbow. It doesn't exist, either.

It has been said that a man who fails to plan plans to fail. One thing I can assure you is that you need to already have your mind made up to succeed. There will be plenty of opportunities to do the same things you did in the past, which will reward you the same results as they did in the past. We must be like Joseph in the Bible. He had his mind made up before he got to Potiphar's house that no matter what or who provoked him, he wasn't going to dishonor God. When you get a moment, read the entire story, and you'll see that he lost his coat, but he maintained his character.

I'm also again reminded of the parable in the Bible of the prodigal son. A man has two sons, and the younger son is ready to get out on his own. One day, he asks his father to give to him now whatever he was going to leave for him when he dies. Yep, very rude and disrespectful. However, the father agrees and does just that. To keep this short, the younger son leaves home with a pocketful of money, goes off, and has himself a good time until his money runs out (you guessed it). His friends run out when the money runs out. The young son finds himself so down and out that he has to take a job feeding swine (hogs). He ends up so broke and hungry that he desires to eat the same thing the hogs are eating. The Bible says one day he comes to himself and realizes where he is, where he has been, and decides at this point that there's no place like home. To keep it even shorter, he makes his way back home, and his father is waiting for him and provides the best he has for him upon his return.

My point is this that if you keep doing the same thing, you're going to keep getting the same thing. Okay, let's do it this way – you and I cannot sow negatively and expect positive results. The Bible says whatsoever a man (woman) soweth, that shall he (she) also reap. Now that we're clear, let's make our way from here.

I don't know where you are at this junction of your life. I don't know how you got where you are or if you're not in a good place. Regardless of the how, who, what, when, why or where, it's time to leave it all behind. Our focus from this point is where we're going, not where we've been.

God is more than ready and prepared to give you the years that the locust, the cankerworm, the caterpillar, and the palmerworm have eaten. While this book was written for the people of Israel, I must admit it is so befitting for our time and lives as well. It reminds to look back at sins, but it also looks reminds to look forward to the future. The people in Israel have slipped back into complacency and apathy about the things of God. Sounds just like us, huh? So, God uses nature, their enemies, and the trails they have faced to awaken them.

One insect after another destroys their crops until there's no food left for the people to eat. Their enemies are strong, numerous, and too power-ful to be stopped. It seems as if they are going to starve to death and utterly be destroyed. But God!

Likewise, God uses various means and meth-ods to accomplish His purpose in our lives. Sometimes He uses the jail cell to lock us up be-fore we're gunned down on the streets or before we shoot someone. It gives us time to think about Him, others, and our own selfish desires. In other words, the writer was right in Romans 8:28 when he said we know all things work together for our good if we love and are called by God for His purpose. God's ultimate goal is to get all of us to a place where we are fit to be used by Him. God will do whatever He needs to do to get our attention.

As I look around me day in and day out, I'm faced with another brother being killed. Often-times, it's one brother killing another brother, or it's another senseless police shooting. It al-most seems as though policemen feel justified to kill since brothers are driving by or pull-ing up and killing each other day and night.

Listen, my brother, there is an "A" in-side of you. You really are awesome!

Let me reiterate so you never forget this: if you didn't have anything to offer Satan, he wouldn't be after you. Satan is actually after what's inside of you, which is greatness! I know it's hard for you to believe that Satan has peeked into your future and that he knows you are a threat every morning your feet hit the floor. You've got to get this. We wrestle not against flesh and blood, but against principalities, against powers, against rulers of darkness, and against spiritual wickedness in high places. The real fight isn't against each other. The real fight is what's inside of each other.

There's an "A" in each of us. We are all awesome.

Satan is always throwing rocks and hiding his hands. Keep in mind the devil is a distractor, divider, deceiver, destroyer, demon, depressor, and a "delusion-arian". You are close enough to put handcuffs on him and put him in your patrol car. My word to all men, and people in general, is always "don't give up, don't give in, and don't give out". Better days are coming. I know it looks rough right now, and I know you've been hearing for a long time that a change is going to come. Don't lose hope. Paul said when he was a child he acted like a child, but when he became a man, he put away childish things. Our timing is not like God's timing. It makes no difference what your color, race, or ethnicity is; all men should be treated right. My primary focus is helping all men live their best life.

Remember this: you are "A"-mazing!

ABOUT THE AUTHOR

In July 2000, **PASTOR LARRY D. JOHNSON** was called to be the Shepherd of Fellowship Missionary Baptist Church. Under the leadership of Pastor Johnson, Fellowship has grown spiritually through true praise and worship. As a result of sound biblical teaching, Fellowship has truly moved from being part of a religion to embodying a personal relationship with God. Pastor Johnson is a native of Marvell, Arkansas, where he was born and raised and finished school. Upon graduating from high school, he moved to Little Rock, Arkansas. His job later transitioned him to Austin, Texas. After residing in Austin for two years, he joined Sweet Home Baptist Church under the auspicious leadership of Dr. Ronald J. Byrd. He then yielded to the Holy

Spirit and accepted his calling to the ministry a year later. He preached his first sermon on Easter Sunday in 1994. The very next year, Pastor Johnson moved back to Arkansas. In 1996, he was elected to be the Pastor of Mt. Olive Missionary Baptist Church in the Marvell community.

In 1998, Pastor Johnson married Holly Willis and from their union came a daughter, Karrington NiKole Johnson. They also have two boys, DeLerick L. Hampton and Raco C. Johnson. After getting married, Pastor Johnson transitioned back to Little Rock, where he attended Philander Smith College. He graduated in May 2002, magna cum laude with a degree in education. He graduated ninth in his class. He was also the Senior Class Chaplain.

He then became an adjunct professor at Philander Smith College for the next three and a half years. He obtained Clinical Pastoral Education (CPE) at Baptist Health Center in Little Rock, Arkansas. After receiving one unit at Baptist Health, he was inspired to go to seminary school for the next six years. He received his doctorate in theology in June 2013.

J. Kenkade
PUBLISHING®

Our Motto
"Transforming Life Stories"

Also Available from J. Kenkade Publishing

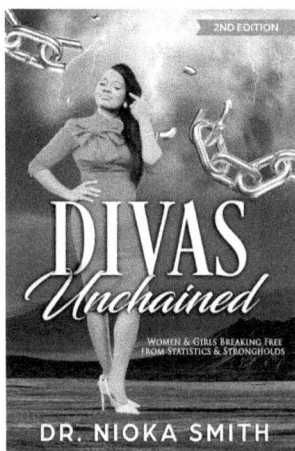

ISBN: 978-1-944486-25-9
Visit www.drniokasmith.com
Author: Dr. Nioka Smith

Sexually abused by her father at the age of 14, pregnant at the age of 17, and a nervous breakdown at the age of 28, Dr. Nioka Smith's painful past almost killed her, until the voice of the Lord guided her into destroying strongholds and reversing Satan's plan for her life. DIVAS Unchained is the powerful chain-breaking reality of the many unfortunate strongholds our women and girls face. Dr. Nioka uses her divine gift to help women and girls break free from destructive life cycles and prosper in all areas of life. Satan has lied to you. It's time to expose his lies. It's time to break free!

Also Available from
J. Kenkade Publishing

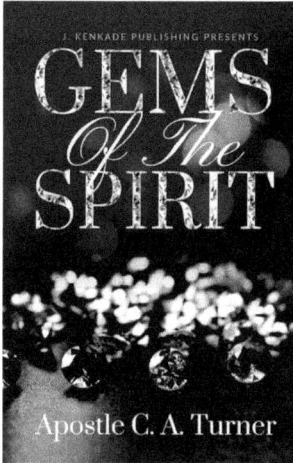

ISBN: 978-1-944486-83-9
Visit www.amazon.com
Author: Apostle C.A. Turner

There's such a hunger for the things of the spirit and the supernatural. Many have decided to tap into the dark side in order to understand more about the Supernatural and the things of the spirit. One of the reasons for this I believe, is because the church as a whole has lost the desire to see a move of God validated by his power with miracles, signs, and wonders. It's my desire and prayer that this information will activate you in ways you never dreamed as you apply it to your spiritual life.

Also Available from J. Kenkade Publishing

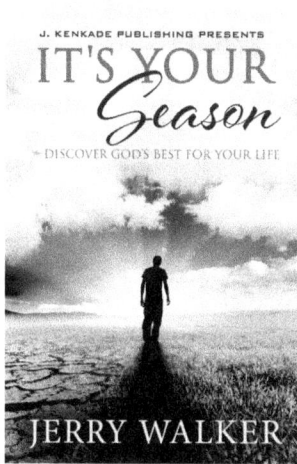

ISBN: 978-1-944486-72-3
Visit www.amazon.com
Author: Jerry Walker

Do you find yourself asking the question, "Is there more to life than the seemingly never-ending struggle of survival?" This book answers that question with a resounding, "YES!" Jesus died to give us MORE. Jerry Walker has written this manual for Christian living that gives in-depth teaching on scripture and how to apply it to your life. Full of tools for living a life of freedom in Christ, this book will be a blessing to all who read it. Your time is now, it truly is your season!

Also Available from
J. Kenkade Publishing

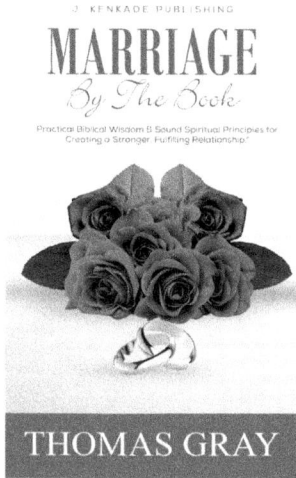

ISBN: 978-1-944486-90-7
Visit www.amazon.com
Author: Thomas Gray

Marriage by the Book is a profound and practical guide-book designed to help you cultivate a deeper relation-ship based on sound Biblical wisdom. Written by Pastor Thomas Gray, this book combines proven step-by-step strategies of practical relationships with spiritual lessons and Bible-based principles to help you overcome conflicts, improve your communication, handle difficult discus-sions, and celebrate the unique union and covenant which unites you together with God. Marriage by the Book is ideal for both new and seasoned couples who are search-ing for better ways to strengthen their relationship and fulfill their promises to God.

www.ingramcontent.com/pod-product-compliance
Lightning Source LLC
La Vergne TN
LVHW051250080426
835513LV00016B/1846